+<=[A Math]~±÷
Journey Through
COMPUTER
GAMES

Hilary Koll & Steve Mills

Crabtree Publishing Company
www.crabtreebooks.com

Crabtree Publishing Company

www.crabtreebooks.com
1-800-387-7650

Published in Canada
616 Welland Ave.
St. Catharines, ON
L2M 5V6

Published in the United States
PMB 59051, 350 Fifth Ave.
59th Floor,
New York, NY

Published in 2016 by CRABTREE PUBLISHING COMPANY.

First published in 2016 by Wayland
(A division of Hachette Children's Books)
Copyright © Wayland 2015

Authors: Hilary Koll and Steve Mills
Commissioning editor: Elizabeth Brent
Editors: Joe Fullman, Rob Colson and Kathy Middleton
Proofreader: Janine Deschenes
Math Consultant: Diane Dakers
Designer: Ed Simkins
Prepress technician: Katherine Berti
Print and production coordinator: Katherine Berti

Production coordinated by Tall Tree Ltd

Photographs:
iStockphoto: 4tl yelet, 4cl colematt, 6-7 Henrik5000,
8-9 dem10, 10tl fcknimages, 10-11 guvendemir,
16-17 Robin Hoood, 18-19 PinkPueblo, 20-21
Zelimir Zarkovic, 22cl CoreyFord, 22bl Naz-3D,
23tr JoeLena, 24tl inides, 26tl carbouval.
Dreamstime: 14tl Chuckchee.
All other images by Shutterstock.

The website addresses (URLs) included in this
book were valid at the time of going to press.
However, it is possible that contents or addresses
may have changed since the publication of this
book. No responsibility for any such changes can
be accepted by either the author or the Publisher.

Printed in Canada/022016/IH20151223

Library and Archives Canada Cataloguing in Publication

Koll, Hilary, author
       A math journey through computer games / Hilary Koll, Steve
Mills.

(Go figure!)
Includes index.
Issued in print and electronic formats.
ISBN 978-0-7787-2311-0 (bound).--
ISBN 978-0-7787-2323-3 (paperback).--
ISBN 978-1-4271-7716-2 (html)

       1. Mathematics--Juvenile literature. 2. Computer games--
Juvenile literature. I. Mills, Steve, author II. Title.

QA40.5.K65 2016   j510   C2015-907935-7
                                          C2015-907936-5

Library of Congress Cataloging-in-Publication Data

Names: Koll, Hilary, author. | Mills, Steve, 1955- author.
Title: A math journey through computer games / Hilary Koll and
     Steve Mills.
Description: New York, New York : Crabtree Publishing, 2016. |
     Series: Go figure! | Includes index.
Identifiers: LCCN 2015049845 (print) | LCCN 2016000172 (ebook)
     ISBN 9780778723110 (reinforced library binding : alk. paper)
     ISBN 9780778723233 (pbk. : alk. paper)
     ISBN 9781427177162 (electronic HTML)
Subjects: LCSH: Computer games--Mathematics--Juvenile literature. |
     Mathematics--Juvenile literature.
Classification: LCC QA76.76.C672 K655 2016 (print) | LCC QA76.76.
     C672 (ebook) | DDC 794.8--dc23
LC record available at http://lccn.loc.gov/2015049845

go figure!

Use your mathematical skills to explore computer games. Solve puzzles and complete missions along the way to become a master gamer!

CONTENTS

04 SCREEN READY

06 HIGH-SPEED DRIVER

08 MONEY MAZE

10 LEADERBOARD SCORES

12 3D CHALLENGE

14 WAR WIZARDS

16 JET FIGHTER

18 ISOLATION

20 AIM AND FIRE

22 ACCURACY RATINGS

24 TRANSFORMING TROOPS

26 SHAPE SHOOTER

28 GO FIGURE! ANSWERS

30 MATH GLOSSARY

32 LEARNING MORE AND INDEX

Words in **bold** appear in the glossary on pages 30–31.

Answers to the Go Figure! challenges can be found on page 28.

Please note: The Imperial and metric systems are used interchangeably throughout this book.

WHAT EQUIPMENT DO YOU NEED?

Pen or pencil

Notepad

Protractor

You might find some of the questions in this book are too hard to do without the help of a calculator. Ask your teacher about when and how to use a calculator.

7 8 9 /
4 5 6 x
1 2 3 +
0 . = -

SCREEN READY

First things first—you need to get your screen set up properly to display the fullest view of the computer games you're playing as well as the best image quality.

LEARN ABOUT IT
RATIOS

Ratios **compare two or more things, such as two lengths. For computer games, the** aspect ratio **describes the relationship between the length and the height of a computer monitor or TV screen.**

Screens display images that are made up of thousands of points called pixels. The length and height of the screen is measured in the number of pixels it can display. For example, a TV screen that has 1280 pixels across (length) and 1024 pixels up (height) has a ratio of 1280:1024.

To figure out the **simplest form** of a ratio, you need to keep dividing each number in the ratio by a number they have in common until you get the smallest whole number possible, as shown in the examples at right.

The same simple ratio can be used to describe several different numbers, as the examples show. So a screen with a ratio of 1280:800 has the same aspect ratio as a screen with the ratio 1680 × 1050.

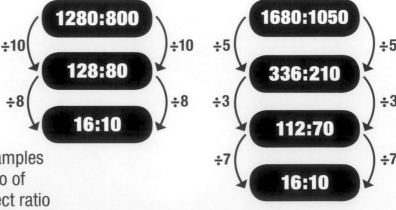

1280:800
÷10 ↓ ÷10
128:80
÷8 ↓ ÷8
16:10

1680:1050
÷5 ↓ ÷5
336:210
÷3 ↓ ÷3
112:70
÷7 ↓ ÷7
16:10

It is easier to compare ratios when the second number is simpified to 1, so the ratio can be written in the form n:1. To do this, divide both numbers in the ratio by the second number. After dividing, the "n," or first number, might end up being a **decimal**.

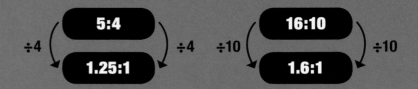

〉GO FIGURE!

The higher the number of pixels your screen has, the clearer the picture will be. Use your knowledge of ratios to figure out the answers to the questions below.

Here are several common aspect ratios for displays.

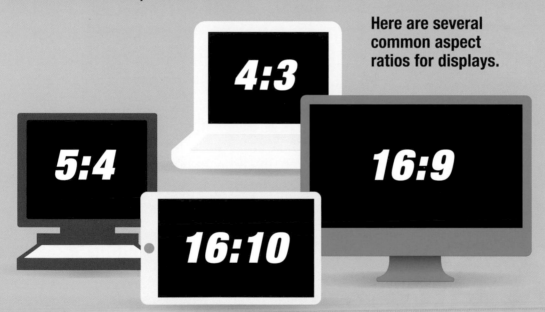

....

1 An old screen has 640×480 pixels.
a) Which of the above aspect ratios is it?
b) Does it have the same aspect ratio as a 1024×768 screen?

2 You look at a screen with 1920 pixels across and 1200 pixels up.
a) Which of the aspect ratios shown above does it match?
b) Write this as a ratio in its simplest form.

3 Many gamers believe that the best ratio for gaming is 16:9. What is this ratio in the form n:1? Use a calculator to help you find n. Round to two decimal places. (See how to round on page 15.)

4 An ultra-high-definition screen has 3840×2160 pixels. Would this be suitable if you wanted to get a screen with the aspect ratio 16:9?

HIGH-SPEED DRIVER

It's time to burn some rubber with this super-speedy driving game. You need to monitor your lap times and speeds to see if you can make it onto the leaderboard. Time to learn some algebra, which is a branch of math that uses formulas to show relationships between things.

LEARN ABOUT IT
SPEED, DISTANCE, AND TIME

06

In algebra, formulas **use letters or symbols to stand in for different things. For example, the formula for finding the time (t) a car takes to travel a certain distance (d) at an average speed (s) can be shown as:**

$$t = d \div s$$ **or** $$t = {}^d\!/_s$$

For example, the time, in hours, it would take a car to go a distance of 6 miles, traveling at an average speed of 120 miles per hour (mph) is:

$$t = 6 \div 120 = 0.05 \text{ hours}$$

Multiply the answer by 60 to find the number of minutes:

$$0.05 \times 60 = 3 \text{ minutes}$$

Multiply this number by 60 to find the number of seconds:

$$3 \times 60 = 180 \text{ seconds}$$

For a car traveling 9 miles at 160 mph:

$$t = 9 \div 160 = 0.05625 \text{ hours}$$

$\times 60$

$$= 3.375 \text{ minutes}$$

$\times 60$

$$= 202.5 \text{ seconds}$$

>GO FIGURE!

Here are two lists on the leaderboards of the players with the fastest lap times for two different tracks:

FAST-LAP PLAYERS' BOARD					
TRACK 7 – DISTANCE 8 MILES			TRACK 8 – DISTANCE 15 MILES		
NAME	TIME (IN SECONDS)	POSITION	NAME	TIME (IN SECONDS)	POSITION
JED	179.5	1	AMY	342.5	1
KIM	182.5	2	JOE	358.5	2
AMY	185	3	JED	386.5	3

1 Here are some of your times for tracks 1 to 5, given in minutes. Write each of these times in seconds: a) 1 minute, b) 1.6 minutes, c) 4 minutes, d) 2.5 minutes, e) 2.8 minutes.

2 You have an average speed of 135 mph driving on track 6, which covers a distance of 9 miles. How long does it take you: a) in minutes, b) in seconds?

3 You record a fast time on track 7, at an average speed of 160 miles per hour. a) How many seconds did it take you? b) Into which position would this get you on the fast-lap players' board?

4 You have made three runs on track 8. Your average speed each time is 135 mph, 160 mph and 180 mph. How many of these laps appear on the players' board and in which positions do they appear?

MONEY MAZE

Learn how to use **coordinates**, or sets of numbers that identify locations on a grid, to guide yourself around the maze and collect some big-money prizes.

LEARN ABOUT IT
FOUR-QUADRANT COORDINATES

08

The grid is divided by two lines called the x-axis (horizontal) and the y-axis (vertical). They divide the grid into four areas called quadrants. The origin is where the x-axis meets the y-axis.

You can refer to any point by giving its coordinates. Coordinates are written as two numbers inside brackets, separated by a comma. The first number shows you the distance you have to go to the left or right across the x-axis to get to a location. The second number shows the distance you have to go up or down on the y-axis.

For example, to reach the point (x,y) on the grid to the right, start at the origin and go 3 squares to the right and 4 squares up. So the coordinates of the point (x,y) are (3,4).

All points on the right of the y-axis have **positive** x **values**. All points on the left of the y-axis have **negative** x values.

All points above the x-axis have positive y values. All points below the x-axis have negative y values. So the point (a,b) is located at the coordinates (-3,-4).

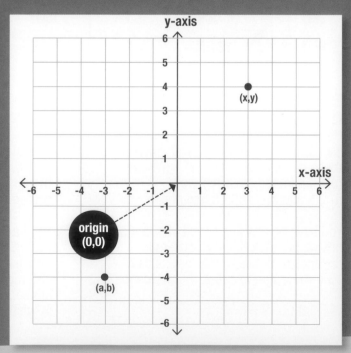

The computer game is showing you this money maze. Find the route that will win you the most money.

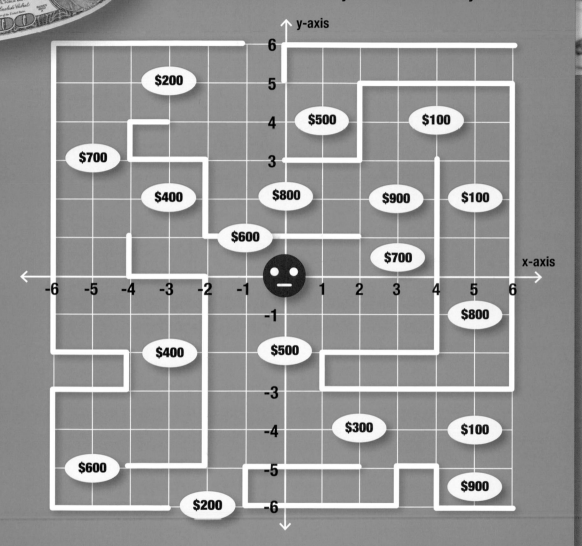

1 Follow each route below. Start at the origin and visit the points, moving along the grid lines. Pick up money in your path. Which route wins you the most money?

Route 1: (0,0) → (0,-4) → (5,-4) → (5,-6)

Route 2: (0,0) → (3,0) → (3,4) → (5,4) → (5,-2)

Route 3: (0,0) → (3,0) → (3,2) → (0,2) → (-3,5) → (-5,5) → (-5,-1) → (-3,-1) → (-3,-3) → (-5,-5)

2 What is your total winnings for the three routes?

LEADERBOARD SCORES

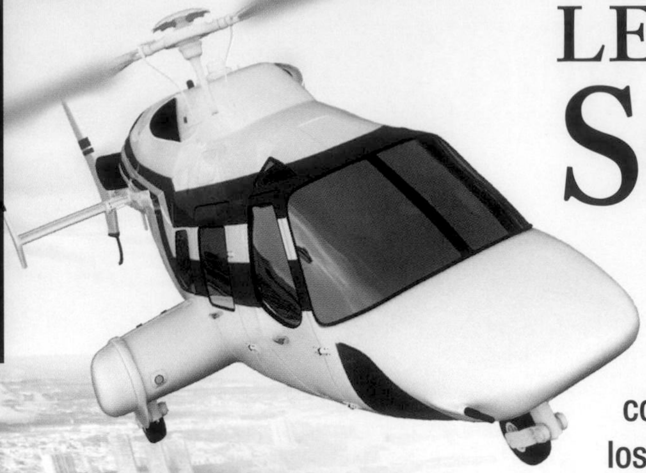

In this game, you must collect points as you travel around a **virtual** city in a news helicopter. For each item you collect (or avoid!) you score points. You lose points for each crash or collision. You can rack up millions of points, so you need to know how to add and subtract large numbers.

LEARN ABOUT IT
LARGE NUMBERS AND PLACE VALUE

When using large numbers, it is important to know the value of the digits and to line them up in columns from the right when adding or subtracting.

We use **place value** to show the number of ones, tens, hundreds, thousands, and so on, that make up a number. We can break numbers down by putting them in columns in a place value chart.

In the example below, we are adding 10,040 (ten thousand forty) to 1,426,709 (one million four hundred twenty-six thousand seven hundred nine). In the place value chart below, you can see we only have to add 1 to the ten-thousands (TTh) digit and 4 to the tens (T) digit to get the answer:

O	Ones
T	Tens
H	Hundreds
Th	Thousands
TTh	Ten thousands
HTh	Hundred thousands
M	Millions
TM	Ten millions
HM	Hundred millions

Millions			Thousands			Ones		
HM	TM	M	HTh	TTh	Th	H	T	O
		1	4	2	6	7	0	9
	+			1	0	0	4	0
	=	1	4	3	6	7	4	9

Subtracting can be done in the same way:

	Millions			Thousands			Ones	
HM	TM	M	HTh	TTh	Th	H	T	O
	2	4	5	8	6	7	9	4
−		1	0	0	2	0	9	0
= 2	3		5	8	4	7	0	4

>GO FIGURE!

You're flying the helicopter through the city following a car on the ground that is driving away from the scene of a robbery. Add and subtract the points for the six actions listed below to get your score.

STARTING SCORE
1,220,694 POINTS

AVOIDED MISSILE
SCORE 15,000 POINTS

COLLIDED WITH BIRD
LOSE 5,100 POINTS

11

LOST TRACK OF CAR
LOSE 120,000 POINTS

NARROWLY MISSED SKYSCRAPER
SCORE 20,400 POINTS

WENT UNDER A BRIDGE WITHOUT CRASHING
SCORE 500,000 POINTS

1 What is your final score?

2 How much more than your starting score is your final score?

3 Will your flight get you onto this leaderboard, and if so, in what position?

RANK	NAME	SCORE
1ST	CLY	1,680,000
2ND	ZTR	1,635,000
3RD	JAY	1,630,999
4TH	DIN	1,630,993
5TH	SAM	1,630,256

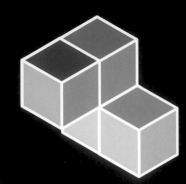

3-D CHALLENGE

For this game, you need to select and match three-dimensional (3-D) shapes made from cubes. Each time you succeed you score points according to the **volume** of each shape.

LEARN ABOUT IT
3-D SHAPES AND VOLUME

3-D shapes, such as cubes, have three dimensions—length, width, and height. The amount of space that a 3-D shape takes up is called its volume.

To find the volume of a cube, multiply its length by its width by its height. Volume is written as the unit of measure, such as centimeters, cubed (cm^3). A 1 cm-high cube has a volume of 1 cm × 1 cm × 1 cm = 1 cm^3

The shape on the left has been drawn on **isometric paper**, which is marked with equally spaced dots to help show dimensions in a drawing. In this example, the volume of each small cube is 1 cm^3. To find the volume of the entire 3-D shape, you can count up the number of cubes. Assuming the two blue cubes are on top of two other cubes, the volume of the whole shape is 10 cm^3.

Viewed from different angles, a 3-D shape can look very different. Sometimes some of the cubes are hidden from view. Here is a shape with a volume of 5 cm^3, viewed from different angles:

We can also turn or flip the shape to see it from other angles, like this:

12

>GO FIGURE!

In this game, you must remove one cube from both of the 3-D shapes in a pair to make the pair identical shapes.

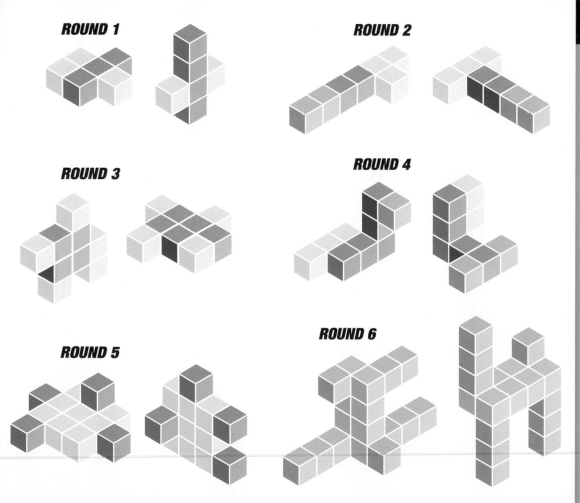

ROUND 1

ROUND 2

ROUND 3

ROUND 4

ROUND 5

ROUND 6

① Doing one round at a time, remove a cube from each shape to leave each pair as two identical shapes.

② Remembering that each small cube has a volume of 1 cm³, find the volume of the final identical shape for each round.

③ You score 1000 points for each 1 cm³ of volume. What do you score for each round?

④ What is your total score for rounds 1 to 6 all together?

WAR OF WIZARDS

Your goal in the *War of Wizards* game is to have the most diamonds. Each wizard tries to turn a box of 100 pieces of stone into diamonds. As a player, you have to buy the wizards. First, you must figure out which wizards are the most reliable at turning stones into diamonds.

LEARN ABOUT IT
PERCENTAGES AND VALUE FOR MONEY

Percentages (%) are fractions with a denominator, or bottom number, of 100. For example, 75% = $^{75}/_{100}$.

If people expect you to get an answer right 75 times out of 100, we can say that you have a reliability percentage of 75 per cent. This can be shown as a diagram. In the diagram on the right, 75 of 100 squares are colored yellow.

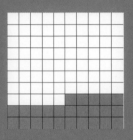

Getting the best value for money means getting the most benefit from a thing for each dollar you spend to buy it. To compare the value for money of items, find out how much you receive of something for each unit of money you spend to buy it. In other words, divide the amount you get by the total price. To compare these bags of gems, divide the weight by the price.

1.24 kg

Cost $10
1.24 ÷ 10
= 0.124 kg per $

1 kg

Cost $8
1 ÷ 8
= 0.125 kg per $

0.6 kg

Cost $5
0.6 ÷ 5
= 0.120 kg per $

In this example, you get more gems for each dollar spent with the 1 kg bag.

To find out which wizard in the game has the best value for money, you need to divide their reliability percentage by their cost. For example:

90%

Cost 50 tokens
90 ÷ 50
= 1.8% per token

54%

Cost 36 tokens
54 ÷ 36
= 1.5% per token

30%

Cost 18 tokens
30 ÷ 18
= 1.67% per token

So, the best value is the first wizard since 1.8 is greater than 1.5 and 1.67.

If a calculator shows a number with many digits after the decimal point, you may want to round the number to make it easier to work with. For example, to round to two decimal places, look at the third digit after the decimal. If it's 5 or more, the second digit goes up 1. If it's 4 or less, the second digit stays the same.

For example:

1.933333333 rounded to 2 decimal places is **1.93**

1.627906977 rounded to 2 decimal places is **1.63**

❯GO FIGURE!

This table shows the reliability percentage rating and cost of each wizard. Each wizard has a box of 100 pieces of stone. You and your enemy have 80 tokens each to buy wizards. You can both buy the same wizard.

WIZARD	RELIABILITY % RATING	PRICE
Warlock	84%	48 tokens
Astra	70%	43 tokens
Shem	60%	34 tokens
Oberon	58%	30 tokens
Japheth	50%	27 tokens
Kasper	48%	25 tokens
Zorn	40%	21 tokens
Filton	33%	18 tokens
Theo	28%	16 tokens

1 If each wizard has 100 pieces of stone to turn into diamonds, how many diamonds would you expect to get from: a) Warlock, b) Astra, c) Japheth, d) Filton?

2 For each wizard in the table, find the value per token you would get (to 3 decimal places). a) Which wizard gives the best value per token.? c) Which wizard gives the least value per token?

3 It costs the same to buy Shem as it does to buy Filton and Theo together. Would you expect to get more diamonds from Shem, or from Filton and Theo combined?

4 Your enemy chooses to buy Astra, Zorn, and Theo with her 80 tokens. How many diamonds would she expect to get altogether?

5 Now choose how to spend your 80 tokens. You don't have to use them all. a) Which combination of wizards will get you the most diamonds for your money? b) How many diamonds would you expect to get?

JET FIGHTER

Your next quest involves flying a supersonic jet as fast and as accurately as possible. Each phase of the game has increasingly difficult challenges and hundredths of a second can win or lose a race.

LEARN ABOUT IT
TIME INTERVALS

Flying times can be shown using colons and decimal points, like this:

3:40.99 means 3 minutes 40 seconds and 99 hundredths of a second.

When time is being added to a digital counter, it is important to remember that 100 "hundredths of a second" (which can be written $^{100}/_{100}$) equals one extra second, 60 seconds equals one extra minute, and 60 minutes equals one extra hour.

3:40.99

minutes	seconds	hundredths of seconds

If you added one hundredth of a second (.01) to the time shown on the left, it flips the hundredths of a second over to "00" and adds one whole second to the seconds (41). So, the new time would be 3:41.00.

3:59.97	3:59.98	3:59.99	4:00.00	4:00.01

This series of timers is showing one hundredth of a second being added each time.

When adding **4:56.40** and **0:00.61**, notice that .40 + .61 equals 101 hundredths of a second. So the number of seconds in the answer is increased by one, with one hundredth of a second leftover, to give **4:57.01**. It can help to stack the times because it puts the numbers in their place value columns.

	4:56.40
+	0:00.61
=	4:57.01

When adding **4:57.01** and **0:03.00**, notice that 57 + 03 equals 60 seconds. So the number of minutes in the answer is increased by one, and the seconds are reduced back to 00, to give **5:00.01**.

```
    4:57.01
+   0:03.00
=   5:00.01
```

When adding **55:59.50** and **0:00.50**, notice that .50 + .50 equals 100 hundredths of a second, so the number of seconds in the answer is increased by one to 60, which, in turn, increases the minutes by one, to give **56:00.00**.

```
    55:59.50
+    0:00.50
=   56:00.00
```

>GO FIGURE!

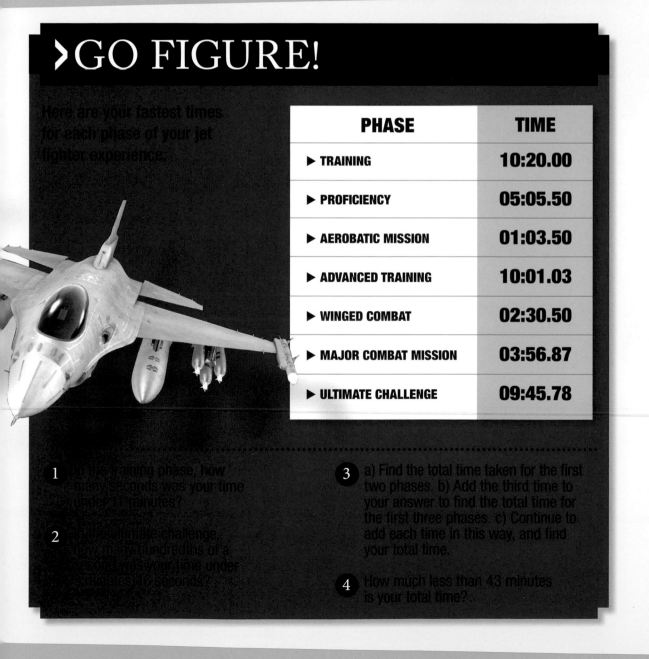

Here are your fastest times for each phase of your jet fighter experience:

PHASE	TIME
▶ TRAINING	**10:20.00**
▶ PROFICIENCY	**05:05.50**
▶ AEROBATIC MISSION	**01:03.50**
▶ ADVANCED TRAINING	**10:01.03**
▶ WINGED COMBAT	**02:30.50**
▶ MAJOR COMBAT MISSION	**03:56.87**
▶ ULTIMATE CHALLENGE	**09:45.78**

1. In the training phase, how many seconds was your time under 11 minutes?

2. In the ultimate challenge, how many hundredths of a second was your time under 9 minutes 46 seconds?

3. a) Find the total time taken for the first two phases. b) Add the third time to your answer to find the total time for the first three phases. c) Continue to add each time in this way, and find your total time.

4. How much less than 43 minutes is your total time?

ISOLATION

For this game, the goal is to isolate a monster alone in one room, while isolating the number the monster is equal to in the room beside it. You must follow special rules to add or remove things equally from the rooms— or the monster will eat you!

LEARN ABOUT IT
SOLVING EQUATIONS

The one main rule is: Any mathematical operation done in one room must also be done in the other. So, if a number is added in one room, the same number must also be added to the other room. The same rule applies if a number is taken out of a room.

For example, to remove the **+7** from the left-hand room shown here, do the inverse, or the opposite, mathematical operation by subtracting 7.

Remember, if we do it to one room, we must also do it to the other.

This leaves us with the monster on its own in the left-hand room and $15 - 7 = 8$ in the right-hand room.

So, the answer is: the monster must equal **8**!

Here is the inverse of different mathematical operations:

Tip: The rule for removing monsters is the same for numbers. If you remove a monster from one room, you must remove one from the other room, too!

›GO FIGURE!

Use the inverse operation method to remove the number from the room with the monster and isolate it.

puzzle 1

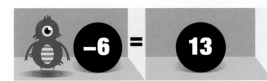

puzzle 2

puzzle 3

puzzle 4

19

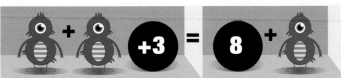

puzzle 5

....

1. Figure out what one monster is equal to for each of these puzzles, using the rules of the game.

2. Make up a similar monster puzzle where the monster is equal to:
a) 6, b) 10, c) 100.

3. Make up a puzzle that has three monsters in one room and two in the other, where each monster is equal to 3.

AIM AND FIRE

For your next game you must learn
how to fire a missile and how to
avoid incoming enemy missiles.

LEARN ABOUT IT
LINEAR GRAPHS

Linear graphs are straight lines shown on a coordinate grid. The coordinates of each point along the straight line share something in common.

Remember, coordinates are always given as the point along the x-axis followed by the point along the y-axis.

20

These coordinates of points appear on the blue dotted line on this grid:
(-5,-4) (-2,-1) (-1,0) (1,2) (3,4) (5,6)

Can you see a pattern in the numbers? The y-coordinate is always equal to the x-coordinate plus 1. We can describe this line using an equation: **y = x + 1**. Every point on the line follows this rule.

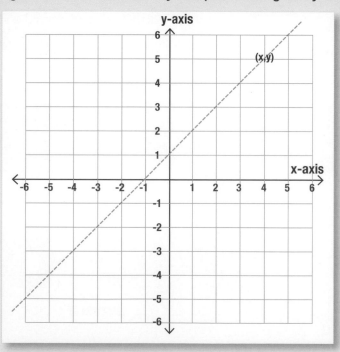

We can also figure out whether other coordinates will fall on this line. For example, (6, 3) is not on the line y = x + 1 since the y-coordinate is not one more than the x-coordinate. We could also replace the value of x in the equation since we know it is 6. The equation becomes y = 6 + 1. The answer, y = 7, does not match the y-coordinate given, which is 3. It is not on the line.

>GO FIGURE!

For this mission you must accurately fire missiles at targets from your fighter jet and avoid enemy missiles.

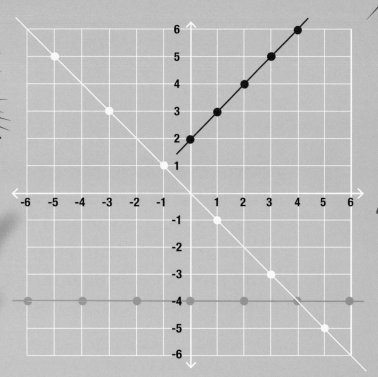

1. You need to program your missile to pass through the following targets, marked in red, on the grid above: (0,2) (1,3) (2,4) (3,5) (4,6).
a) Look at the coordinates and write down the pattern of the x- and y-coordinates.
b) What equation would you use to program the missile?

2. a) Write the coordinates of the targets marked in green on the grid above.
b) What pattern do you notice about the y-coordinate of each of the points along the green line?

3. a) Write the coordinates of the targets marked in yellow on the grid above.

b) What do you notice about the x- and y-coordinates of each of the points along the yellow line?
c) Which of these equations would result in the yellow path?
$y = x$, $y = 2x$, $y = 5$, $y = -x$.

4. A missile has been programmed using the equation $y = x - 3$. Complete the coordinates to show points along the missile's path:
a) (5,?), b) (3,?),
c) (-2,?), d) (-3,?).

5. If you are at (2,-1), do you need to take action to avoid the missile from question 4?

ACCURACY RATINGS

The game *Dinopotomas* tests your skills in moving around a world of dangerous creatures. Players' scores are calculated as percentages to give a rating on how accurate they are.

LEARN ABOUT IT
FRACTIONS AND PERCENTAGES

Parts of a whole can be written as fractions. In a fraction, the number representing the whole is on the bottom and is called the denominator. The number representing a part is on the top and is called the numerator.

For example, if you scored 200 points out of a total of 800 points in a game, this can be written as the fraction $^{200}/_{800}$. Fractions can then be written in their simplest form by dividing both numbers by the largest number they have in common to give a smaller fraction. Here, both numbers can be divided by 200 to get the fraction ¼.

Sometimes it is easier to divide several times to reach the simplest form.

$$\frac{200}{800} \overset{\div 200}{\underset{\div 200}{=}} \frac{1}{4}$$

$$\frac{77}{140} \overset{\div 7}{\underset{\div 7}{=}} \frac{11}{20}$$

$$\frac{3060}{7650} \overset{\div 10}{\underset{\div 10}{=}} \frac{306}{765} \overset{\div 3}{\underset{\div 3}{=}} \frac{102}{255} \overset{\div 51}{\underset{\div 51}{=}} \frac{2}{5}$$

Fractions can also be expressed as percentages, which are easier to compare. To write a fraction as a percentage, you must first multiply the denominator by the number that will make it equal 100. The numerator must also be multiplied by the number multiplied against the denominator. The percentage is the top number of the answer. Here are some examples:

$$\overset{\times 25}{\frac{1}{4}} = \frac{25}{100} = 25\% \qquad \underset{\times 25}{}$$

$$\overset{\times 5}{\frac{11}{20}} = \frac{55}{100} = 55\% \qquad \underset{\times 5}{}$$

$$\overset{\times 20}{\frac{2}{5}} = \frac{40}{100} = 40\% \qquad \underset{\times 20}{}$$

>GO FIGURE!

These accuracy ratings have been calculated by finding the percentage of mistakes a player made out of the total number of tasks performed.

PLAYER	NUMBER OF MISTAKES	TOTAL NUMBER OF TASKS	MISTAKES AS FRACTION	FRACTION IN SIMPLEST FORM	%	ACCURACY RATING (100% - PERCENTAGE)
JHK	200	800	$\frac{200}{800}$	$\frac{1}{4}$	25%	75%
SID	8	40				
PET	50	200				
DAN	9	100				
JUL	34	200				
ZAK	21	75				

1. Copy out the table and complete it by calculating the accuracy ratings for:
a) SID, b) PET, c) DAN, d) JUL, e) ZAK.

2. Which two players have the same accuracy rating?

3. a) Who has the highest accuracy rating?
b) Who has the lowest accuracy rating?

4. Write the players in order, starting with the player with the highest accuracy rating.

5. If you only made 6 mistakes out of a total of 150, how much better would your accuracy rating be than the best of the other players? Give your answer as the number of percentage points.

TRANSFORMING TROOPS

In the game *Ancient Civilization*, you are responsible for ordering where the troops in your army should go. You must give accurate directions to your troops to ensure that your civilization is not destroyed.

LEARN ABOUT IT
GEOMETRICAL TRANSLATIONS AND PYTHAGOREAN THEOREM

24

In math, translations are made when you slide a shape without turning or flipping it. You can slide a shape horizontally, vertically, or diagonally.

When describing a translation that moves on a diagonal, we say how many units the shape slides across and how many units it slides up or down. If we draw lines to follow the direction of movement horizontally, veritcally, and diagonally, it creates a **right-angled triangle**, shown at right.

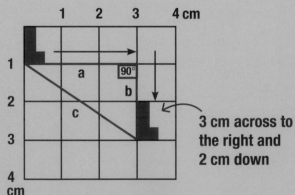

3 cm across to the right and 2 cm down

The **Pythagorean theorem** gives information about the relationship between the sides of a right-angled triangle. It states that the **square number** of the long, diagonal side is equal to the sum of the square numbers of the two shorter sides. This is shown by the formula:

$$a^2 + b^2 = c^2$$

In the diagram above, **a** and **b** are the shorter sides and **c** is the diagonal (also called the hypotenuse).

We can use the Pythagorean formula to find the squared length of the diagonal line, using the horizontal and vertical lengths, like this:

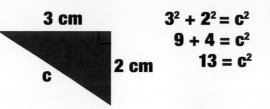

3 cm

2 cm

c

$3^2 + 2^2 = c^2$
$9 + 4 = c^2$
$13 = c^2$

To find the value of c, we have to find the square root of c^2. On a calculator, use the square root sign ($\sqrt{\ }$) to find the value of c.

$\sqrt{13} = c$, so **c = 3.6 cm**
(rounded to one decimal place)

›GO FIGURE!

You want your troops to go to different cities on this map. Remember that each square is 1 cm and represents 1 km.

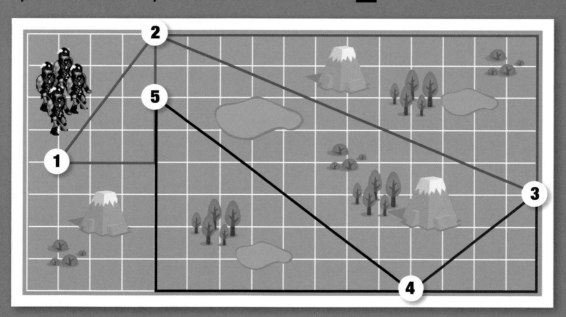

1. You must first order your troops to move from 1 to 2. Use the green triangle to help you describe the translation to move your troops. Give the number of kilometers, and whether to move left or right, or up or down.

2. Use the Pythagorean theorem to figure out the length of the diagonal line from 1 to 2 to tell your troops how far to march.

3. Give the order for moving from 2 to 3, describing the translation in terms of horizontal and vertical distances. Use the Pythagorean theorem to figure out the diagonal distance that the troops must march.

4. Repeat the steps in question 3 for marches from a) 3 to 4, b) 4 to 5.

5. What is the total marching distance for your troops if they march from 1 to 5 following the diagonal lines shown?

SHAPE SHOOTER

On your final mission, you must destroy dangerous fragments of a recently-exploded space station that are falling through the stratosphere. This mission is vital to save the world!

LEARN ABOUT IT
ANGLES AND QUADRILATERALS

Angles are measured in degrees (°). We measure angles with a tool called a protractor, like the one shown below.

An angle that is 90 degrees (90°) is called a right angle. An angle less than 90° is called an **acute angle**. Angles between 90° and 180° are called **obtuse angles**. To measure and draw angles, line up the center of the protractor with the corner of the angle, like this:

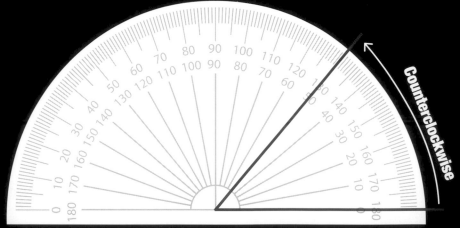

Counterclockwise

Be careful to start from zero on each side of the protractor. Measured in a counterclockwise direction, this angle is 50° (not 130°).

Quadrilaterals are two-dimensional (2-D) shapes with four straight sides.

Below are examples and definitions of special types of quadrilaterals:

Parallelogram: Two sets of **parallel** lines (a, b, c, d).

Rectangle: Four right angles. It is a type of parallelogram (a, d).

Square: Four right angles and four sides of equal length; It is a type of rectangle (d).

Rhombus: Two sets of parallel lines and four sides of equal length. It is a type of parallelogram (c, d).

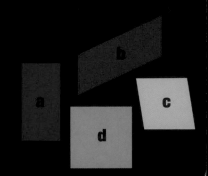

Trapezium: One set of parallel lines. One of the parallel lines is longer than the other (e, f).

Kite: Two short sides **adjacent** and of equal length, and two longer ones adjacent and of equal length (g, h).

If a shape with four straight sides doesn't match any of the descriptions, we just call it a quadrilateral (i).

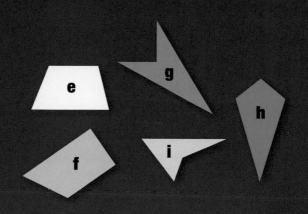

❯GO FIGURE!

Calculate the angles necessary to aim your missiles so they hit and destroy the fragments before they fall to Earth.

Tip: When measuring counterclockwise, measure with the inside numbers. When measuring clockwise, measure with the outer numbers.

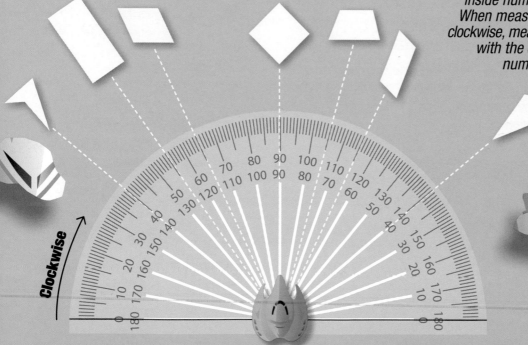

1 If you set a missile to be fired at 90° to the horizontal line of your spacecraft, what fragment shape of the exploded space station would you hit?

2 Reading the angles in a clockwise direction, is it true that firing at 115° would hit a parallelogram?

3 Through what clockwise angle should you set the missile to fire to hit:
a) the (non-square) rectangle,
b) the trapezium?

4 What fragment shape would you hit if you fired at a clockwise angle of 140°?

GO FIGURE! ANSWERS

04–05 Screen ready
1. a) 640:480 = 4:3 b) 1024:768 = 4:3, so it does have the same ratio
2. a) 1920:1200 = 16:10 b) 16:10 = 8:5
3. 16 ÷ 9 = 1.78, so the ratio is 1.78:1
4. Yes

06–07 High-speed driver
1. a) 1 × 60 = 60 seconds
   b) 1.6 × 60 = 96 seconds
   c) 4 × 60 = 240 seconds
   d) 2.5 × 60 = 150 seconds
   e) 2.8 × 60 = 168 seconds
2. a) 9 ÷ 135 = 0.066 × 60 = 4 minutes
   b) 4 × 60 = 240 seconds
3. a) 8 ÷ 160 = 0.05 × 60 = 3 × 60 = 180 seconds b) Second
4. Two would appear: 300 seconds would be first, 337.5 seconds would be second

28

08–09 Money maze
1. Route 1: 500 + 300 + 100 + 900 = $1800
   Route 2: 700 + 900 + 100 + 100 + 800 = $2600
   Route 3: 700 + 900 + 800 + 200 + 700 + 400 + 600 = $4300
2. 1800 + 2600 + 4300 = $8700

10–11 Leaderboard scores
1. 1,220,694 + 15,000 − 5100 − 120,000 + 20,400 + 500,000 = 1,630,994
2. 1,630,994 − 1,220,694 = 410,300
3. Yes, fourth

12–13 3-D Challenge
1.

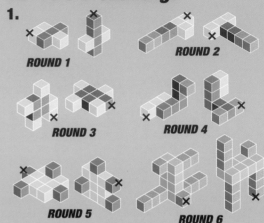

ROUND 1   ROUND 2
ROUND 3   ROUND 4
ROUND 5   ROUND 6

2. 5 cm³, 6 cm³, 8 cm³, 8 cm³, 12 cm³, 17 cm³
3. 5000, 6000, 8000, 8000, 12,000, 17,000
4. 5000 + 6000 + 8000 + 8000 + 12,000 + 17,000 = 56,000

14–15 War of wizards
1. a) 84 b) 70 c) 50 d) 33
2. a) Warlock 84 ÷ 48 = 1.750
   Astra 70 ÷ 43 = 1.628
   Shem 60 ÷ 34 = 1.765
   Oberon 58 ÷ 30 = 1.933
   Japheth 50 ÷ 27 = 1.852
   Kasper 48 ÷ 25 = 1.920
   Zorn 40 ÷ 21 = 1.905
   Filton 33 ÷ 18 = 1.833
   Theo 28 ÷ 16 = 1.750
   b) Oberon c) Astra
3. Shem has a reliability percentage of 60, but Filton and Theo have a combined percentage of 61, so they would produce the most diamonds
4. 70 + 40 + 28 = 138 diamonds
5. a) Oberon, Kasper and Zorn will get you the most for a cost of 76 tokens (30 + 25 + 21) b) 146 (58 + 48 + 40)

16–17 Jet fighter

1. 40 seconds
2. 22 hundredths of a second
3. a) 10:20.00 + 05:05.50 = 15:25.50
   b) 15:25.50 + 01:03.50 = 16:29.00
   c) 16:29.00 + 10:01.03 + 02:30.50 + 03:56.87 +
      09:45.78 = 42:43.18
4. 16.82 seconds

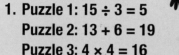

18-19 Isolation

1. Puzzle 1: $15 \div 3 = 5$
   Puzzle 2: $13 + 6 = 19$
   Puzzle 3: $4 \times 4 = 16$
   Puzzle 4: remove a monster
   from each to leave 9
   Puzzle 5: remove a monster
   from each, then $8 - 3 = 5$
2. Answers will vary
3. Answers will vary

20–21 Aim and fire

1. a) The y-coordinate is always 2 more than
      the x coordinate. b) $y = x + 2$
2. a) (-6,-4) (-4,-4) (-2,-4) (0,-4) (2,-4)
      (4,-4) (6,-4)
   b) The y-coordinate is always -4.
3. a) (-5,5) (-3,3) (-1,1) (1,-1) (3,-3) (5,-5)
   b) The x- and y-coordinates have the
      opposite sign: when x is positive, y is
      negative, and vice versa
   c) $y = -x$
4. a) (5,2) b) (3,0) c) (-2,-5) (-3,-6)
5. Yes

22–23 Accuracy ratings

1. a) SID: $\frac{8}{40} = \frac{1}{5} = 20\%$ $100 - 20 = 80\%$
   b) PET: $\frac{50}{200} = \frac{1}{4} = 25\%$
   $100 - 25 = 75\%$
   c) DAN: $\frac{9}{100} = 9\%$
   $100 - 9 = 91\%$
   d) JUL: $\frac{34}{200} = \frac{17}{100} = 17\%$
   $100 - 17 = 83\%$
   e) ZAK: $\frac{21}{75} = \frac{28}{100} = 28\%$
   $100 - 28 = 72\%$
2. JHK and PET
3. a) DAN b) ZAK
4. DAN, JUL, SID, JHK and PET, ZAK
5. $\frac{6}{150} = \frac{4}{100} = 4\%$ $100 - 4 = 96\%$,
   so your accuracy would be
   5 percentage points better than
   the best score

24–25 Transforming troops

1. 3 km to the right, 4 km up
2. $3^2 + 4^2 = 9 + 16 = 25$, $\sqrt{25} = 5$ km
3. 12 km to the right and 5 km down
   $12^2 + 5^2 = 144 + 25 = 169$
   $\sqrt{169} = 13$ km
4. a) $3 \to 4$: 4 km left and 3 km down
      $4^2 + 3^2 = 16 + 9 = 25$, $\sqrt{25} = 5$ km
   b) $4 \to 5$: 8 km left and 6 km up
      $8^2 + 6^2 = 64 + 36 = 100$
      $\sqrt{100} = 10$ km
5. $5 + 13 + 5 + 10 = 33$ km

26–27 Shape shooter

1. Square
2. Yes
3. a) 55°, b) 105°
4. Kite

MATH GLOSSARY

ACUTE ANGLE
An angle that is less than 90°

ADJACENT
Two sides of a shape are adjacent if they share the same angle.

ANGLE
The amount of turn, measured in degrees

ASPECT RATIO
The ratio between the width and height of a shape

COORDINATES
A series of numbers that will locate a point against axes

DECIMAL
A number with a decimal point in it. The digit to the left of the decimal point is the number of units, while the digit to the right is the number of tenths.

EQUATION
A statement that says two things on either side of an equals sign are equal. Equations are solved by entering values.

FORMULA
An equation that shows the relationship between two different quantities

ISOMETRIC PAPER
Paper marked with equally spaced lines or dots to help you draw pictures of 3-D shapes and some 2-D shapes

LINEAR GRAPH
A graph that shows the relationship in which the amount goes up or down in the same amount each time, forming a straight line. It is sometimes called a straight-line graph.

NEGATIVE NUMBERS
A number that is less than zero. We write negative numbers using the minus sign (-), e.g. -5, -3, -7.

OBTUSE ANGLE
An angle that is between 90° and 180°

OPERATION
A mathematical process carried out on one or more numbers to produce another number. The four most common operations are addition, subtraction, multiplication, and division.

PARALLEL
Lines or shapes that never meet and are always the same distance apart

PERCENTAGE
A percentage is a special fraction which has a denominator of 100, e.g. 42% = $^{42}/_{100}$. Per cent means "for every hundred."

PLACE VALUE
The value that a digit has based on where it appears in a number

POSITIVE NUMBERS
Numbers that are greater than zero

PROTRACTOR
A mathematical instrument, shaped in a circle or a semi-circle. It is marked with degrees and is used to measure angles.

PYTHAGOREAN THEOREM
The square of the long side of a right-angled triangle (the hypotenuse) is equal to the sum of the squares of the other two sides. This can be written as $a^2 + b^2 = c^2$, where a and b are the two shorter sides and c is the hypotenuse.

QUADRANT
One of the four sections created when a grid is divided by two lines that cross, such as the x-axis and y-axis

RATIO
Ratios show how one or more numbers or values are related to another. So a ratio of 2:1 shows that there are twice as many of the first value as there are of the second.

RIGHT-ANGLED TRIANGLE
A triangle that has a right angle, 90°, as one of its angles.

SIMPLIFY/SIMPLEST FORM
To simplify a fraction, we change it to an equivalent fraction that uses smaller numbers, e.g. $\frac{6}{8} = \frac{3}{4}$. When a number cannot be simplified, it is in its simplest form. Ratios can also be simplified in the same way, 4:12 = 1:3.

SQUARE NUMBER
The number we get by multiplying a number by itself, written using the symbol ^{2}. So 2^2 means 2×2, 3^2 means 3×3, and so on.

SQUARE ROOT
The number that creates a given squared number when multiplied by itself

VALUE
The total amount that a number or group of numbers adds up to

VIRTUAL
An imitation of something on a computer

VOLUME
The amount of space an object takes up. It is measured in cubic units, such as cubic centimeters (cm^3) or cubic meters (m^3).

LEARNING MORE

WEBSITES

www.mathisfun.com
A huge website packed full of explanations, examples, games, puzzles, activities, worksheets, and teacher resources for all age levels.

www.khanacademy.org
A learning resource website for all ages, it contains practice exercises and easy-to-follow instructional videos on all subjects, including math.

www.mathplayground.com
An action-packed website with math games, mathematical word problems, worksheets, puzzles, and videos.

INDEX

32

addition 10–11
angles 26–27
average 6–7

coordinates 8–9, 20–21

decimal 5
decimal points 15, 16
decimal places 15
denominator 14, 23
distance 6–7

equations 18–19

fractions 22–23

hypotenuse 24

inverse 18, 19

kite 27

linear graphs 20–21

negative values 8

operation 19

parallelogram 26, 27
percentages 14–15, 22–23
place value 10
positive values 8
protractor 26
Pythagorean theorem 24–25

quadrants 6
quadrilaterals 26–27

ratios 4–5
rectangle 26, 27
rhombus 26
right-angled triangles 24–25

shapes 12–13
simplest form 4
speed 6–7
square (shape) 26
squares 24
square root 25
subtraction 10–11

time intervals 16–17
three-dimensional (3D) 12–13
translations 24–25
trapezium 27

value for money 12–13
volume 12–13